An Abstract of the Thesis Entitled

# The Military Discipline of the Romans from the Founding of the City to the Close of the Republic

## By

GEORGE W. CURRIE, Ph.D.,

*Professor of Latin and Greek, Birmingham Southern College*

Originally published under the auspices of the Graduate Council of Indiana University

**1928**

An Abstract of the Thesis Entitled

# The Military Discipline of the Romans from the Founding of the City to the Close of the Republic

## By

## GEORGE W. CURRIE, Ph.D.,

*Professor of Latin and Greek,*
*Birmingham Southern College*

Originally published under the auspices of the Graduate Council of Indiana University in **1928.**

**Published by**

S zeteo Enterprises
συζητεο πραγματων

**2017**

*An Abstract of the Thesis Entitled* **The Military Discipline of the Romans from the Founding of the City to the Close of the Republic**

By GEORGE W. CURRIE, Ph.D.,

ISBN 978-1936830-99-2

**Note:**

# Preface

The chronological summary of punishable military offenses here given presents an abstract of a fuller discussion of the cases deposited in the library of Indiana University in type written copies of the entire thesis.

To avoid multiplication of references to the sources, those only have been included here which give the most direct evidence on the cases.

For suggestions leading to the choice of the subject I am indebted to Professor S. E. Stout as well as for numerous suggestions from his inspiring classroom and encouraging consultations.

**George Currie**

# Contents

General Introduction                                                      1

I. Chronological Summary of Punishable Military Offenses

    1. The Early Period                                    4
    2. The Punic Wars Period                               8
    3. The Late Republican Period                         16

II. General Conclusions Based on Total Data Regarding      29
    Punishable Military Offenses

    1. Mutiny                                             30
    2. Insubordination of Individuals                     31
    3. Disorderliness                                     31
    4. Laxness                                            32
    5. Criminality                                        32
    6. Desertion                                          33
    7. Miscellaneous Cases                                36
    8. Conclusions                                        36

III. The Nature of Military Discipline of the Romans as    38
    Indicated by General Statements of the Sources

    1. The Early Period                                   38
    2. The Punic Wars Period                              42
    3. The Late Republican Period                         45
    4. From Vegetius and The Digest                       48

Bibliography                                                             50

List of Abbreviations                                                    53

# GENERAL INTRODUCTION

Modern writers on the subject of public antiquities of the Romans have usually emphasized the strictness of Roman military discipline but occasionally a dissenting voice[1] has raised a question as to the strict rigor practiced by the Romans in dealing with their soldiers. The purpose of this discussion is to state the facts in the matter in an exhaustive study of the sources of our knowledge.

The generally accepted sense of the word discipline is training to act in accordance with established rules, but the discussions of military discipline are usually confined to training to obey military authority by punishment of guilty soldiers. In the first division of this study, the material from the sources is merely set forth in this narrow sense. In the second division, the conclusions based on the first are given together with a comparison of different periods of Roman history. The periods of history adopted are: the Early Period, from the founding of the city to the Punic wars (753-264);[2] the Punic Wars Period (264-146); the Late Republican Period (146-31).

The method used here attempts to separate opinion from fact. First, we shall give the results of a study of the actual events of Roman history that pertain to the punishment of opposition to military law and authority. Then we shall include statements and opinions of ancient authorities that are indicative of fact. The first of these two tasks is not without difficulty. Sometimes an intended breach of discipline or an intended punishment was not wholly carried out. For example, soldiers may have intended to retreat from battle to their camp without orders and the commander may have intended to slay them if they persisted, in which case the intent must be taken as an indication of the law and practice in the matter. Sometimes authors disagree as to facts, in which case the most probable statement, when everything is considered, must be taken for fact.

For the sake of convenience in focusing a variety of offenses to one general conclusion, six general classifications are used here: Insubordination, including mutiny or concerted in subordination and individual insubordination; Disorderliness, including insolence, disobedience, rioting, etc.; Laxness, such as negligence, slowness to respond to orders and indul-

---

[1] v. William Stewart Messer in Classical Philology, 1920.
[2] All dates in this thesis are B.C. unless otherwise indicated.

gence in luxury; Criminality, such as murder, plunder, and theft; Desertion of three kinds—going over to the enemy, leaving one's post or the signa, and retreat without orders (cowardice) ; Punishments mentioned without statement of the offense. The last are classed as miscellaneous. It is not always possible to distinguish with entire clearness in making these classifications; for example, it is difficult to say in some cases of rioting whether or not they reached a stage of mutiny, or to distinguish between the three types of desertion. But cases of doubt are comparatively few and do not affect the truth of the general conclusions.

Another difficulty arises in distinguishing what to include and what to reject as military discipline. It should be under stood that evasion of the draft was punished by civil law. In a few instances punishment of a military offense was carried out by vote of the people. These instances have been included. Results varying with interpretation of other doubtful factors will be mentioned where they are concerned.

**Note:** Dates written as 672/640 indicate an occurrence sometime between the two.

# I. CHRONOLOGICAL SUMMARY OF PUNISHABLE MILITARY OFFENSES

## 1. THE EARLY PERIOD

| Case | B.C. | Commander | Offenders | Offense | Circumstances | Outcome |
|---|---|---|---|---|---|---|
| 1. | 672/ 640 | Tullus Hostilius | Mettius Fufetius and Albans | Desertion and treachery. | In Roman army as allies | Mettius scourged and torn asunder between chariots; accomplices slain |
| 2. | 509 | Tarquinius Superbus | Roman army | Revolt and expulsion of king | Soldiers ratify revolt of the city | No punishment as Tarquinius never regained power |
| 3. | 499 | A. Postumis | Roman soldiers | Running in battle | Battle of Lake Regillus | Fleeing soldiers ordered to face enemy or be killed |
| 4. | 494 | T. Veturius | Roman soldiers | Insolence | Consul forced to engage against will | No mention of discipline |
| 5. | 494 | T. Veturius A. Verginius | Roman Armies | Mutiny | Withdrawal to Sacred Mount | Amnesty granted |
| 6. | 483 | L. Valerius | Roman army | Laxness | War against Volscians; general envied by the soldiers | No punishment |
| 7. | 481 | Caeso Fabius | Roman Infantry | Disobedience | Refuse to pursue Veientes and retreat without orders | No punishment; general obliged to close the campaign |
| 8. | 471 | App. Claudius | Roman army | Desertion of Post, insubordination, loss of arms and standards | War against Volsci | Centurions and standard bearers scourged and beheaded; privates decimated |
| 9. | 458 | L. Minucius, cos.; Cincinnatus, dictator | Roman army | Cowardice | Aequi besiege camp | Army rebuked and deprived of spoils; general reduced to a legatus |
| 10. | 455 | Romilius, consul | Siccius and followers | Mutiny | Consul sends them on dangerous exploit purposely | No punishment except dishonor to consuls |
| 11. | 450/ 449 | Decemvirs M. Cornelius L. Minucius M. Sergius T. Antonius K. Duilius | Five legions | Mutiny and deserting commanders | Second secession to Sacred Mount | No punishment; loss of command by the decemvirs |
| 12. | 450/ 449 | L. Siccius | Roman escort | Murder by conspiracy with decemvirs | Civil strife carried to military affairs | Avenged with death or exile of the decemvirs by civil law |

4

# PUNISHABLE MILITARY OFFENSES

*References*

1. Dion. Hal. *Antiq*. Rom. III. 24-34; Liv. I. 27. 28; Ampel. XXXIX. 2

2. Liv. I. 59-60; Dion. Hal. *Antiq. Rom.* IV. 67.3; 85; Eutr. I. 8; Plut. *Pop.* I . 3

3. Liv. II. 20; Dion. Hal. *Antiq. Rom.* VI. 5. 4-13

4. Liv. II. 31; Dion. Hal. *Antiq. Rom.* VI. 42-43

5. Dion. Hal. *Antiq. Rom.* VI. 45. 2; VI. 48. 1; Liv. II. 32. 1-3

6. Dion. Hal. *Antiq. Rom.* VIII. 89. 3

7. Liv. II. 43; Dion. Hal. *Antiq. Rom.* IX. 3.; IX. 9. 4; Zon. 7. 17

8. Liv. II. 58-59; Dion. Hal. *Antiq. Rom.* IX. 50. 3-7; App. II. 7; Zon. 7. 17; Front. *Strat*. IV. 1. 34 cf. *Dig*. 49. 16. 6. 3

9. Liv. III. 26. 3-29. 3; Dion. Hal. *Antiq. Rom.* X. 25; Val. Max. II. 7. 7 cf. Flor. I. 5. 12; Eutr. I. 17; Oros. II. 12. 7-8

10. Dion. Hal. *Antiq. Rom.* X. 36-39. 1; 40-47

11. Liv. III. 42; 50-54; Dion. Hal. *Antiq. Rom.* XI. 23; 44; Diod. XII. 4; Eutr. I. 18: Ampel. XXV. 2

12. Liv. III. 43; Dion. Hal. *Antiq. Rom.* XI. 25-27

| Case | B.C. | Commander | Offenders | Offense | Circumstances | Outcomes |
|---|---|---|---|---|---|---|
| 13. | 450/ 449 | Decemvirs<br>Q. Fabius<br>Q. Petilius<br>M. Rabuleius | Three Legions | Mutiny and deserting commander | Second Secession to Sacred Mount | No punishment; loss of command by the decemvirs |
| 14. | 431 | A. Postumius | His son | Leaving post to conquer enemy | In hard-fought battle with the Aequi and Volsci | Put to death with the axe |
| 15. | 423 | C. Semproniu | Roman army | Laxness | General over-confident | No punishment |
| 16. | 418 | Q. Servilius dictator | A standard bearer | Lagging in a charge | Battle with Aequi and allies | Slain by the dictator in line |
| 17. | 414/ 413 | M. Postumius | Roman army | Quaestor struck and general killed | After campaign against Aequi; friction between general and army | A few punished by death by civil law |
| 18. | 396 | Camillus | Deserters | Left camp | Siege of Vei | Punished |
| 19. | 393 | Sp. Postumius | Roman army | Flee from enemy | Advance into territory of Aequi | Severely rebuked; ask to be led at once to battle |
| 20. | 393 | C. Aemilius | Roman army | Flee from fear | Uncertain report of defeat of comrades near by | No mention |
| 21. | 390 | Q. Sulpicius | Guards | Asleep on duty | Citadel of Rome attacked at night by Gauls | Guard at fault hurled from cliff |
| 22. | 381 | Camillus | Roman | Cowardice | War with the Volsci | Reprimanded only |
| 23. | 358 | C. Sulpicius, dictator | Roman army | Laxness in obedience | Campaign against Gauls | No mention of punishment |
| 24. | 343/ 342 | C. Marcius Rutilus, cos.<br>Cn. Corvinus, dictator | Roman Guards | Criminal plot and insurrection | Detection and intended punishment turns into prospective civil war | Cause of plot removed by cancelling debts; dismissed from service |
| 25. | 340 | T. Manlius | His son | Fought against orders | Latin revolt; cavalry commander challenged him | Son put to death by father order |
| 26. | 325 | L. Papirius Cursor, dictator | Fabius Rullianus | Fought against orders | Dictator absent; war against Sabines | Fabius condemned to death but pardoned |
| 27. | 325 | L. Papirius, dictator | Roman soldiers | Purposely lagged in battle | Disaffection on account of the affair of Fabius | General adopted milder course and promised booty |
| 28. | 322/ 295 | Fabius Rullus | Two legions | Cowardice | Yielded post | Those chosen by lot slain |

## References

13. Liv. III. 42; 50-51; Dion. Hal. *Antiq. Rom.* XI. 23; 44; Diod. XII. 4

14. Diod. XII. 64. 3; Liv. IV. 29. 5-6; Val. Max. II. 7. 6

15. Liv. IV. 37. 6-41. 9; Val. Max. III. 2. 8; VI. 5. 2

16. Liv. IV. 46-47. 4; Front. *Strat.* II. 8.

17. Liv. IV. 50-51. 3; Zon. 7. 20; cf. Diod. XIII. 38. 1; Flor. I. 22. 2

18. Liv. V. 19. 4; cf. Plut. *Cam.* 5; Flor. I. 6. 12; cf. *Dig.* 49. 16. 3. 11; 49. 16 5. 1-3

19. Liv. V. 28. 5-13

20. Liv. V. 28. 5-13

21. Liv. V. 47, 7ff; Plut. *Cam.* 27 .5 cf. Dig. 49. 16. 10. 1; 49. 16. 3. 6

22. Liv. VI. 24. 4-7; VIII. 23. 15

23. Liv. VII. 12. 7-15. 8

24. Liv. VII. 38. 5-41; App. III. 1-2; Zon. 7. 25 fin.; Aur. Vic. *Vir.Ill.* 29. 3 cf. Front. *Strat.* I. 9. 1

25. Liv. 6. 16-8. 2; Val. Max. II. 7. 6; Front. *Strat.* IV. 1. 40; Dion. Hal. *Antiq. Rom.* II. 26. 6; VIII. 79. 2; Flor. I. 14; Oros. III. 9. 1-4; Dio VII. 35. 2-9; Zon. 7. 26; Aur. Vic. *Vir. Ill.* 28. 4; Cic. *De Off.* III. 31. 112fin; *De Fin.* I. 7. 23; Cell. IX. 13. 20; Sall. *Cat.* 52. 30 cf. Liv. VIII. 12. 1

26. Liv. 8. 30-35. 9; Val. Max. II. 7. 8; III. 2. 9; Front. *Strat.* IV. 1. 39; Dio VIII. 36. 1-7; Aur. Vic. *Vir. Ill.* 31. 1-4; 32. 1; Eutr. II. 8 cf. *Dig.* 49. 16. 3. 15 and Pauly-Wissowa on Fabius No. 114

27. Liv. VIII. 35. 10-36

28. Front. *Strat.* IV. 1. 35

2—43551

| Case | B.C. | Commander | Offenders | Offense | Circumstances | Outcome |
|---|---|---|---|---|---|---|
| 29. | 302 | M. Aemilius Paulus | Roman army | Flight and loss of signa | War against Etruscans; foragers ambuscaded | Forced to camp outside ramparts without tents |
| 30. | 294 | M. Atilius Regulus | Roman Cohort | Flight to camp | War against Samnites | Ordered killed or return to fight, which they did |
| 31. | 280/279 | P. Valerius Levinus | Romans | Defeat without good reason | War with Pyrrhus | Ordered by senate to winter in tents |
| 32 | 280 | P. Valerius Levinus | Romans | Cowardice | Surrender with arms in war against Pyrrhus | Degradation |
| 33 | 280/271 | L. Genucius | Guards | Slay Rhegians | Garrison to protect Rhegium | Survivors scourged and beheaded at Rome and dead bodies dishonored |

## 2. THE PUNIC WARS PERIOD

| Case | B.C. | Commander | Offenders | Offense | Circumstances | Outcome |
|---|---|---|---|---|---|---|
| 1. | 263 | Otacilius Crassus | Roman soldiers | Surrender with arms | War with Hannibal in Sicily | Required to camp outside rampart |
| 2. | 260 | Cn. Scipio Asina | Crew of fleet | Mutiny and desertion | General deceived | No mention of punishment |
| 3. | 256 | M. Attilius Regulus | Mannius, military tribune | Leading a mutiny | First expedition to Africa against Carthage | Threatened with death |
| 4. | 252 | C. Aurelius Cotta | Valerius tr. mil. | Disobedience | War in Sicily | Flogged |
| 5. | 252 | C. Aurelius Cotta | P. Aurelius Pecuniola | Negligence | In command at siege of Lipara | Beaten and reduced to private in infantry |
| 6. | 252 | C. Aurelius Cotta | Equites | Disobedience | War in Sicily; knights ordered to work | Branded by censors; pay denied by decree of senate and people |
| 7. | 249 | P. Claudius Pulcher | Soldiers Roman and Allied | ? | Siege of Lilybeum | Severely punished; allied flogged |
| 8. | 218 | P. Cornelius Scipio | Gauls— 2000 pedites; 200 equites | Desert to enemy | Just before Battle of Trebia | No punishment |
| 9. | 218 | Cn. Scipio | A few prefects of a fleet | Negligence | Surprised and defeated by Hasdrubal | Punishment |
| 10. | 218 | L. Manlius, praetor | Roman army | Mutiny | Operations in Gaul | No mention |

## References

29. Liv. X. 3. 6-4. 5

30. Liv. X. 36. 1-12; Front. *Strat*. IV. 1. 29; II. 8. 11

31. Front. *Strat*. IV. 1. 24; Zon. 8. 5

32. Eutr. II. 13. 2; Val. Max. II. 7. 15; Front. *Strat*. IV. 1. 18; Zon. 8. 4; Liv. *Epit*. 13; Liv. XXV. 6. 1-3

33. Polyb. I. 7. 5-13; App. 9. 1-3; Val. Max. II. 7. 15; Liv. XXVIII. 28. 2-4; Liv. *Epit*. 12; 15; Front. *Strat*. IV.1. 38; Oros. IV. 3. 3-5; Zon. VIII. 6 fin; Dio IX. 7-12

### Punic Wars Period

1. Front. *Strat*. IV. 1. 19

2. Polyb. I. 21; Zon. 8. 10 fin.; Eutr. II. 20. 2; Oros. IV. 7. 7; Liv. *Epit*. 17; Polyaen. VI. 16. 5; Flor. II. 2; Val. Max. VI. 6. 2; Ampel. 46 cf. Zon. 8. 11

3. Flor. II. 2. 17

4. Front. *Strat*. IV. 1. 30

5. Front. *Strat*. IV. 1. 31; Zon. 8. 14; Val. Max. II. 7. 4

6. Front. *Strat*. IV. 1. 22

7. Diod. *Fr*. 3. Bk. 24; Polyb. I. 49

8. Liv. XXI. 48. 1-3; Polyb. III. 67

9. Polyb. III. 76; Liv. XXI. 61. 1-4

10. Liv. XXII. 33. 7; XXIII. 21. 7

| Case | B.C. | Commander | Offenders | Offense | Circumstances | Outcome |
|------|------|-----------|-----------|---------|---------------|---------|
| 11. | 217 | Q. Fabius Maximus | Minucius | Insubordination | Campaign against Hannibal | Minucius given equal power, failed and returned to obedience |
| 12. | 216 | C. Teremtius Varro | Roman soldiers | Disobedience | Consuls disagree about pursuit to plunder; ambush reported awaiting | No punishment; Varro to blame |
| 13. | 216 | Fabius Maximus | A Lucanian | Absent without leave | After Cannae when Fabius was attempting to hold Rome's allies from deserting | Cause removed without punishment |
| 14. | 216/ 206 | P. Sempronius Tuditanus, tr. Mil. | Roman Soldiers | Cowardice | Just after Battle of Cannae | Ransom refused to 7000; others kept in undesirable service indefinitely |
| 15. | 214 | Q. Fabius, cos. | 370 Roman deserters | Desertion to revolting towns | Italian cities had gone over to Hannibal | Flogged and thrown from Tarpeian Rock |
| 16. | 214 | T. Otacillius | Naval Allies | Desertion | Mercenaries desert to Syracuse, an independent state | No mention |
| 17. | 214 | M. Marcellus | Roman allies | Desertion | To Leontini | 2000 put to death |
| 18. | 214 | Ti. Gracchus | Soldier slaves | Cowardice | Battle against Hanno | Granted citizenship then punished; must stand while eating |
| 19. | 212 | Cn. Fulvius Flaccus | Army of 18000 | Disobedience; do as please | In Apulia against Hannibal; Fulvius fled with 200 | 2000 survivors assigned service in Sicily with those from Cannae; given barley for seven years; Fulvius exiled |
| 20. | 212/ 211 | Senate and people | L. Marcius | Insubordination | Assumed command and title "proprietor" by election of soldiers | Deposed (from command) |
| 21. | 211 | Q. Fulvius | Allied deserters | Desertion | Capture of Capua by the Romans | Hands cut off |
| 22. | 210 | Scinio and Laelius | Soldiers and marines | Rioting over war decorations | After capture of New Carthage | Quieted by good management |

11. Liv. XXII. 23-30; Polyb. III. 90-104; App. VII. 12-16; Dio XIV. 57. 8-19; Zon. 8. 25-26; Plut. *Fab*. Max. 4-13; *Apophth*. 2, *Comp*. *Per. el Fab*. 2-3; Val. Max. III. 8. 2; V. 2. 4; Front. *Strat*. I. 8. 2; II. 5. 22; Aur. Vic. *Vir. Ill*. 43; Nep. *Hann*. 5. 1-3; Polyaen. *Exc*. 46. 10; Sil. Ital. VII. 1. 90ff.; 272ff; 381ff;515ff.

12. Liv. XX. 42; App. VII. 18

13. Plut. *Fab. Max*. 20

14. Liv. XXII. 50; 53. 12-54; 61. 3; XXIV. 18. 9; XXV. 5. 10; XXVI. 9. 4; XXIX. 24. 11; Front. *Strat*. IV. 5.7; 7. 39; IV. 1. 44; Val. Max. II. 7. 15; V. 6. 7; Plut. *Marcel*. 13; Sil. Ital. X. 426; Dio XV. 57. 28

15. Liv. XXIV. 20 cf. Liv. XXIII. 12. 16; Veg. *Rei Mil*. II. 5

16. Liv. XXIV. 23. 10; cf. Liv. 11. 9

17. Liv. XXIV. 30. 6; Plut. *Marcel*. 14

18. Liv. XXIV. 14-16; Flor. II. 6-30; Val. Max. V. 6. 8

19. Liv. XXV. 21; Val. Max. II. 8. 3

20. Liv. XXV. 37. 5; XXVI. 2; Val. Max. II. 7. 15; I. 6. 2; VIII. 15. 11; Front. *Strat*. II. 6. 2; 10. 2; Sil. Ital. XIII. 700

21. App. VII. 43; Liv. XXVI. 33. 3

22. Liv. XXVI. 46. 4; Dio XVI. 42; Zon. IX. 8

3—13551

| Case | B.C. | Commander | Offenders | Offense | Circumstances | Outcome |
|------|------|-----------|-----------|---------|---------------|---------|
| 23. | 209 | Marcellus | Routed army | Cowardice and loss of some standards | Battle against Hannibal | All reprimanded cohorts losing signa given barley; their centurions stand in without belts and withdrawn swords for a time |
| 24. | 208 | Salapians,Rom. allies | 601 Latin Speaking deserters | Desertion | Hannibal uses them as advance guard to get in allied town by deceit | Ruse discovered; the deserters slain |
| 25. | 206 | Scipio Africanus | 8000 soldiers and 35 ring leaders | Mutiny | Scipio sick; suspense of operations with delayed pay | 35 ringleaders beheaded; others compelled to re new oath |
| 26. | 205 | Pleminius, Rom. commander at Locri | Two tribunes Mutin and soldiers | Mutiny | Fight over stolen cup; Pleminius mutilated | Tribunes beaten; later trial at Rome anticipated by being mobbed; Pleminius later imprisoned and died |
| 27. | 205 | Senate | Roman Soldiers | Theft from temple | Roman guard at Locri | Restoration twofold decreed or death sentence would follow |
| 28. | 204 | Scipio Africanus | Soldiers | Disobedience and murder | Locha capitulated; granted terms | Soldiers deprived of booty; guilty captains made to cast lots publicly; three put to death |
| 29. | 203 | Scipio Africanus | Spaniards | Plot to burn Roman camp | Serving Romans under compulsion | Guilty put to death |
| 30. | 203/ 201 | Scipio Africanus | Deserters | Desertion | Terms proposed, accepted and carried out demand deserters | Latin deserters beheaded; Roman crucified |
| 31. | 199 | P. Villius, COS. | 2000 veterans | Mutiny | Called volunteers; claimed they had been compelled to enroll | Reprimanded and promised adjustment |
| 32. | 195 | M. Cato | Rom. troops | Lagging | Hurried pursuit of enemy | The consul himself struck or ordered centurions to strike laggers |
| 33. | 195/ 194 | M. Cato | A soldier | Neglect of duty | Left by departing fleet on enemy shore | Punished |

## References

23. Liv. XXVII. 12. 9-13. 13; Plut. *Marcel*. 25; Oros. IV. 18. 4

24. App. VII. 51; Liv. XXVII. 28; Zon. 9. 9; Front. *Strat*. IV. 7. 38

25. Polyb. XI. 27-30; Dio XVI. 57. 47; Zon. IX. 10; App. VI. 34; Liv. XXVIII. 24-30

26. Liv. XXIX. 9; 19. 6-8; XXXIV. 44. 7; Diod. XXVII. 4; App. VII. 55; *Zon*. 9. 11 Val. Max. I. 1. 21

27. Diod. XXVII. 4; Liv. XXIX. 19. 6-8; cf. references under no. 26

28. App. VIII. 15

29. App. VIII. Pt. I. 29-30

30. Liv. XXX. 37. 3; 43. 11; Zon. 9. 14; App. VIII. 54; Val. Max. II. 7. 12; Eutr. III. 21 fin.

31. Liv. XXXII. 3

32. Liv. XXXIV. 15

33. Front. *Strat*. IV. 1. 33

| Case | B.C. | Commander | Offenders | Offense | Circumstances | Outcome |
|---|---|---|---|---|---|---|
| 34. | 194 | M. Cato | Lacetanians give up 600 deserters | Desertion | Lacetanians subdued; end of Cato's command in Spain | Put to death |
| 35. | 190 | M. Aemilius | Roman soldiers | Cowardice | Flight from Eumenes' troops | Tribune left in charge of camp stationed men to kill refugees to camp; they return to fight |
| 36. | 190 | L. Aemilius Regillus, praetor | Roman soldiers | Plundering against orders | Capture of Phoeaea | No mention of punishment |
| 37. | 192/ 185 | M. Cato, censor | L. Quinetius Flaminius | Crime | War in Gaul; had man slain at feast | Expelled from senate |
| 38. | 187 | Cn. Manlius Vulso | Army | Laxness | War against Antiochus | No punishment |
| 39. | 180 | A. Postumius Albinus | M. Fulvius and his legion | Insubordination; unauthorized discharge i.e. desertion | Campaign among Ligures | Fulvius exiled to Farther Spain; soldiers returned receive half pay. Army not returning were to be sold and goods confiscated |
| 40. | 177 | C. Claudius Pulcher | Officers and soldiers | Disobedience and disrespectful language | Consul went to Instria to command without taking auspices or insignia of office | Discharge, hence no share of spoils |
| 41. | 176 | Q. Petilius Spurinus | A legion | Allowing the consul to be killed | War in Liguria | Deprived of pay and credit for the campaign |
| 42. | 171 | P. Licinius Crassus | Deserter | Desertion | War with Perses; the deserter furnished king information | No mention; probably thrown under elephants in 167 |
| 43. | 169 | Aemilius Paulus | Officers and soldiers | Laxness | War with Perses | Unpunished but reformed |
| 44. | 168 | Aemilius Paulus | Cretan deserter | Desertion | War with Perses | No mention; probably thrown under elephants |
| 45. | 147 | Scipio Aemilianus | Roman army | Laxness | Siege of Carthage | Unpunished but reformed |
| 46. | 146 | Scipio Aemilianus | Roman and allied deserters | Desertion | Fall of Carthage | Romans burned themselves; allied thrown to beasts in gladiatorial shows |

## References

34. Plut. *Cato* 11; Liv. XXXIV. 43. 8; Nep. *Cato* 2

35. Liv. XXXVII. 43. 1-4; App. XI. 36; Justin XXXI. 8

36. Liv. XXXVII. 32

37. Liv. XXXIX. 42. 10 ff.; Liv. *Epit*. 39; Cic. *Cato Major* 12. 42; Val. Max. II. 9. 3; Plut. *Cato* 17; Aur. Vic.*Vir*. III. 47. 4

38. Liv. XXXVIII. 50. 4; ff.; XXXIX. 6. 3; cf. Polyb. XXIII. 14. 1-4, 7-11; Diod. XXIX. 21

39. Liv. XL. 41 cf. Front. *Strat*. IV. 1. 32; Val. Max. II. 7. 5; Gell. *Noct. Att*. V. 6. 24; Vel. Pat. I. 10. 6 (cf. Liv. XLI. 27 Müllers ed.)

40. Liv. XLI. 10

41. Val. Max. II. 7. 15; Front. *Strat*. IV. 1. 46; Liv. XLI. 18. 11

42. Liv. XLII. 65. 2; Val. Max. II. 7. 14; cf. Val. Max. II. 7. 15

43. Liv. XLIII. 14; XLIV. 1. 5; Zon. IX. 23. 1; Liv. XLV. 35-37; Plut. *Aem*. Paul. 30

44. Polyb. XXIX. 15; Plut. *Aem*. Paul. 16; Val. Max. II. 7. 14

45. App. VIII. 115

46. App. VIII. 130-131; Polyb. XXXIX. 4; Val. Max. II. 7. 13 cf. Dig. 49. 16. 4. 1

# 3. THE LATE REPUBLICAN PERIOD

| Case | B.C. | Commander | Offenders | Offense | Circumstances | Outcome |
|------|------|-----------|-----------|---------|---------------|---------|
| 1. | 145 | Fabius Aemilianus | Celtiberi | Desertion | Roman garrison duty | Hands cut off |
| 2. | 142 | Quintus Macedomicus | Five legionary cohorts | Loss of post | Siege of Spanish town | Punished by perilous service |
| 3. | 140 | Caepio | Cavalry | Attempt to burn commander | Cavalry sent on dangerous duty | Commander routed; no mention of punishment |
| 4. | 140 | Q. Pompeius | Deserters | Desertion | Proposed terms of surrender | No mention |
| 5. | 138 | Brutus or Popillius | C. Matienius | Desertion | Service in Spain | Flogged and sold for a sesterce |
| 6. | 137 | Sex. Brutus | Deserters | Desertion | Demand deserters as terms of surrender | No mention |
| 7. | 134 | Scipio Aemilianus | Roman army | Laxness | Siege of Numantia | Reproof and strenuous exactions |
| 8. | 133 | L. Calpurnius Piso | Cavalry | Cowardice | Surrender of arms | Degradation |
| 9. | 132 | P. Rupilius | Q. Fabius | Negligence | Loss of citadel | Dishonorably discharge |
| 10. | 110 | Aulus Albinus | Centurions and auxiliaries | Desertion | Corrupted by enemy | No mention |
| 11. | 109 | Q. Metellus | Roman soldiers | Lax discipline | War against Jugurtha | Severe punishment |
| 12. | 108 | Metellus | Turpilius | Surrender | Suspicion of disloyalty | Put to death |
| 13. | 108 | Metellus | Ligurians and Thracians | Desertion | Jugurtha gave over deserters to the Romans | Hand cut off or half buried, speared and burned |
| 14. | 102 | Catulus | Roman fleet | Flee post | War against Cimbri | Roman general regains control by strategy |
| 15. | 97 | Didius and Sertorius | Roman garrison | Laxness | Wintering at Castulo, Spain; on garrison duty | Unpunished but mostly slain by enemy |
| 16. | 90 | C. Papius Mutilus | 2000 Romans | Desert to enemy | Choose service with enemy rather than death; Social war | No mention |
| 17. | 90 | Sex. Julius Caesar | Many Numidians | Desertion | Their captive king displayed by enemy | Those remaining discharged |
| 18. | 89 | Aul. Postumius Albinus | Roman navy | Slay Roman commander | General accused of corruption | No mention |

## References

1. Vel. Pat. II. 5; Front. *Strat.* IV. 1. 42; Val. Max. II. 7. 11

2. Vel. Pat. II. 5; Val. Max. II. 7. 10; Front. *Strat.* IV. 1. 23

3. Dio XXII. 78; *Frag. ox.* Obseq. 195 cf. App. VI. 70-74; Liv. *Epit.* 54; Liv. *Epit.* 67

4. App. VI. 79; Val. Max. VIII. 5. 1; Flor. II. 18; Val. Max. II. 7. 1; Front *Strat.* IV. 1. 1; Liv. *Epit.* 54; Vell. Pat. II. 1; Diod. *Frag.* 1. XXXIII

5. Front. *Strat.* IV. 1. 20

6. App. VI. 73; *Liv. Epit.* 55; 59; Flor. II. 17; Eutr. IV. 19

7. App. VI. 85-86; Front. *Strat.* IV. 1. 1; Val. Max. II. 7. 1; Flor. II. 18. 9; Eutr. IV. 17. 2; Liv. *Epit.* 57; Plut. *Apophth. Scip. Min.* 16; Polyaen. 8. 16. 2; Veg. III. 10. fin.

8. Val. Max. II. 7. 9; Front. *Strat.* IV. 1. 26

9. Val. Max. II. 7. 3

10. Sall. *Jug.* 38. 6

11. App. VIII. pt. II. 2; Sall. *Jug.* 44 ff.; Val. Max. II. 7. 2; Front. *Strat.* IV. 1-2; Eutr. IV. 27. 1-2

12. Plut. *Pomp.* 11; 14. 5; Front. *Strat.* IV. 5. 1; Zon. 10. 3; Plut. *Apophth. Reg. et. Imp.* 6

13. Sall. *Jug.* 66-69; App. VIII. pt. II. 3; Plut. *Mar.* 8; Val. Max. II. 10. 1; App. B. C. I. 31

14. Plut. *Mar.* 23; Val. Max. V. 8. 4; Front. *Strat.* IV. 1. 13

15. Plut. *Ser.* 3

16. App. B. C. I. 42; Flor. III. 18; Liv. *Epit.* 73

17. App. *B. C.* I. 42

18. Plut. *Sulla* 6. 8-9; Val. Max. IX. 8. 3; Liv. *Epit.* 75; Oros. V. 18. 22; Polyaen. VIII. 9. 1

| Case | B.C. | Commander | Offenders | Offense | Circumstances | Outcome |
|------|------|-----------|-----------|---------|---------------|---------|
| 19. | 89 | L. Porcius Cato | Veterans | Throw clods at general | Attempt to exact work and obedience | Ringleader arrested but escaped punishment |
| 20. | 88 | L. Cornelius Sulla | Superior officers | Desert | When marching on Rome in civil war | No mention |
| 21. | 88 | Sulla | Roman Soldiers | Looting | Civil war | Punished |
| 22. | 88 | Sulla | Roman Soldiers | Slay officers | Civil war | No mention |
| 23. | 88 | Q. Pompeius | Soldiers | Slay general | Civil war | Rebuked by a general; general of faction opposing slain |
| 24. | 87 | Cinna | Ex-slave soldiers | Plunder and Murder | Civil war | Put to death |
| 25. | 87 | Sulla | Roman troops | Not mentioned | Mithradatic war in Greece | Disgrace |
| 26. | 87 | Octavius | Army in Rome | Desertion | Civil war | No mention |
| 27. | 87 | Strabo | Roman soldiers | Revolt and plan murder of commander | Commander selfish and suspected of disloyalty to the state | 800 desert; rest reconciled |
| 28. | 86 | Sulla | Roman soldiers | Cowardice | Campaign against Archilaus | Chastisement and work |
| 29. | 86 | Flaccus | Roman Soldiers | Riotous | Mithradatic war | Punished |
| 30. | 86 | Flaccus | Fimbria | Insubordination | Flaccus inexperienced; employed Fimbria's aid | Offender discharged |
| 31. | 86 | Thermus | Roman soldiers | Rebellious | Corrupted by discharged officer | Commander routed |
| 32. | 85 | Sulla | Deserters | Desertion | Terms offered Mithradates | Punished |
| 33. | 84 | Cinna | Roman soldiers | Desertion | Civil war | No mention |
| 34. | 84 | Cinna | Roman soldiers | Mutiny | Civil war | Commander slain |
| 35. | 83 | L. Scipio | Roman soldiers | Desertion | Civil war | No punishment |
| 36 | 82 | Carbo | Five cohorts | Desertion | Civil war | No punishment |
| 37. | 82 | Carbo | 500 Celtiberian horse | Desertion | Civil war | No punishment |

## References

19. Dio XXXI fr. 100 cf. Flor. III. 18; Liv. *Epit*. 75; Vell. Pat. II. 164

20. App. B. C. I. 56-57

21. App. *B. C.* I. 59

22. Plut. *Sulla* IX. 1; Vell. Pat. II. 18

23. App. *B. C.* I. 63; Vell. Pat. II. 20: Liv. *Epit*. 77

24. App. *B. C.* I. 74; Plut. *Ser*. 3 fin.

25. App. XII. 32; Front. *Strat*. IV. 1. 27

26. Plut. *Mar*. 42. 3

27. Plut. *Pomp*. 3. 1-3 cf. Vell. Pat. II. 21. 2; Plut. *Pomp*. 1. 3; Liv. *Epit*. 79; App. *B. C.* I. 68; Obseq. 116

28. Plut. *Sulla* 16. 5

29. App. XII. 52

30. Dio XXXI. 104; App. XII. 52; Aur. Vic. *Vir. Ill*. III. 70. 2

31. App. XII. 52

32. App. XII. 55; Vell. Pat. II. 23. 6

33. App. *B. C.* I. 78; Liv. *Epit*. 83

34. App. *B. C.* I. 78; Liv. *Epit*. 83; Plut. *Pomp*. 5; Vell. Pat. II. 24. 5

35. App. *B. C.* I. 85; Plut. *Sulla* 28. 2-3; Flor. III. 21; Vel. Pat. II. 25; Diod. *Fr. Bk*. 37

36. App. *B. C.* I. 88

37. App. *B.C.* I. 89

4—43.151

| Case | B.C. | Commander | Offenders | Offense | Circumstances | Outcome |
|---|---|---|---|---|---|---|
| 38. | 82 | Marcius | Eight legions | Desertion | Civil war | No punishment |
| 39. | 82 | Carbo | 1000 soldiers | Desertion | Civil war | No punishment |
| 40. | 82 | Albinovanus | Legion | Desertion | Civil war | No punishment |
| 41. | 82 | Norbanus | Albinovanus and Lucanians | Desert and slay officer | Civil war | Escape to enemy |
| 42. | 81 | Pompeius Magnus | Soldiers | Disorderliness | On march | Punished |
| 43. | 81 | Domitius Ahenobarbus | 7000 soldiers | Desertions | Civil war | No punishment |
| 44. | 81 | Pompeius Magnus | Roman army | Disorderliness | Treasure hunting | No punishment |
| 45. | 78 | Brutus | Roman army | Mutiny | Civil war | No punishment |
| 46. | 76 | Sertorius | One cohort | Inclined to disrespect women | Siege of a town | Put to death |
| 47. | 76 | C. Curio | A legion | Rebellious | War with the Dardani | Degraded and disbanded |
| 48. | 74 | Lucullus | Asiatic army | Lawless and stubborn | Mithradatic war | Punished |
| 49. | 74 | Sertorius | Spanish army | Inclined to desert | Civil war | Punished |
| 50. | 72 | Sertorius | Perpenna | Insubordination | Civil war | Unpunished |
| 51. | 72 | Perpenna | Army | Rebellious | Civil war | Some rewarded; some punished or threatened; some killed |
| 52. | 71 | M. Crassus | Two legions | Cowardice | War with Spartacus | Decimation |
| 53. | 67 | Lucullus | Asiatic army | Mutiny and desertion | Different accounts | No punishment |
| 54. | 67 | ? | Romans | Desertion | In Mithradates' army | No mention but fear punishment |
| 55. | 58 | Caesar | Army in Gaul | Seditious | Fear Ariovistus | No punishment but rebuke |
| 56. | 55 | Crassus | Ignatius and 300 horse | Desertion | Disaster | No punishment |
| 57. | 55 | Crassus | Army | Disloyal | Retread and disagree on policy | Slain by enemy |
| 58. | 54 | Caesar | Dumnorix and allied horsemen | Desertion | Dumnorix tried to start revolt | Dumnorix slain; horsemen brought back |
| 59. | 52 | Caesar | Soldiers and centurions | Rashness | Siege of Gergovia | Army reprimanded |

# References

38. App. *B. C.* I. 90

39. App. *B. C.* I. 91

40. App. *B. C.* I. 91

41. App. *B. C.* I. 91

42. Plut. *Pomp.* 10. 7; cf. 20. 4

43. Plut. *Pomp.* 11. 1-4

44. Plut. *Pomp.* 11 cf. Plut. *Pomp.* 14. 5; Front. *Strat.* IV. 5. 1; Zon. 10. 3; Plut. *Apophth. Reg. el Imp.* 6

45. Plut. *Pomp.* 16. 1-6; Zon. 10. 2

46. App. *B. C.* I. 109

47. Front. *Strat.* IV. 1. 43

48. Plut. *Lucull.* 7 cf. App. XII. 52

49. App. *B. C.* I. 111-112

50. App. *B. C.* I. 114; Flor. III. 22; Vell. Pat, II. 30; Plut. *Ser.* 26

51. App. *B. C.* I. 114; Flor. III. 22; Vell. Pat. II. 30; Plut. *Ser.* 26

52. App. I. 118-119; Plut. *Crass.* 10. 2

53. Dio 36. 14-17 cf. Plut. *Pomp.* 31. 5-6; Dio 36. 46; App. XII. 90

54. App. XII. 98; 110-111 cf. Plut. *Ser.* 24. 3

55. Caes. *B. G.* I. 39; Dio 38. 35; 38. 37; 38. 47; Front. *Strat.* I. 11. 3; IV. 5. 11

56. Plut. *Crass.* 27. 7-8

57. Plut. *Crass.* 31. 1-5

58. Caes. *B. G.* V. 6-7

59. Caes. *B. G.* VII. 45. 8-9; 47. 3; 52.

| Case | B.C. | Commander | Offenders | Offense | Circumstances | Outcome |
|------|------|-----------|-----------|---------|---------------|---------|
| 60. | 49 | Thermus | Five cohorts | Desertion | Civil war | No punishment |
| 61. | 49 | Attius Varus | Garrison | Desertion | Civil war | No punishment |
| 62. | 49 | Lentulus Spinther | Ten cohorts | Desertion | Civil war | No punishment |
| 63. | 49 | Q. Lucretius and Attius, a Pelignian | Seven cohorts | Desertion | Civil war | No punishment |
| 64. | 49 | Dominitius Ahenobarbus | 35 cohorts | Desertion | Civil war | No punishment |
| 65. | 49 | Rutilius Lupus | Three cohorts | Desertion | Civil war | No punishment |
| 66. | 49 | Petreius | Light armed and auxiliaries | Desertion | Lack of supply | No punishment possible |
| 67. | 49 | Petreius | Army | Inclined to desert | Civil war | Punished with cruelty |
| 68. | 49 | M. Varro | A legion of soldiers born in Spain | Desertion | Civil war | No punishment |
| 69. | 49 | Caesar | Army | Mutiny | Civil war | Leaders put to death; others dismissed |
| 70. | 49 | Curio | Two centurions and 22 Men | Desertion | Civil war | No punishment |
| 71. | 48 | Pompeius Magnus | Soldiers from Epirus and Vicinity | Desertion | Civil war; on forced march | No punishment possible |
| 72. | 48 | Caesar | Two Gallic Chiefs | Desertion | Civil war | Escaped to enemy |
| 73. | 48 | Caesar | Some soldiers | Desertion | Civil war | No mention |
| 74. | 48 | Caesar | Army | Cowardice | Civil war | Degradation of leaders (The army requests decimation.) |
| 75. | 48 | Pompey | Septimius, his assassin | Desertion | ? | No mention |
| 76. | 48 | Cassius Longinus | Legion of soldiers born in Spain, Marcellus and two cohorts | Desertion and mutiny | Hatred of general, resulting in revolt and open civil war | Attempted punishment by open war on the revolters but finally settlement peaceably |
| 77. | 47 | Sallust | Army of Caesar | Mutiny | Awaiting action | Some dismissed; some exposed to danger later |
| 78. | 46 | Caesar | Caesar's army | Riotous | Complaint against Caesar's luxury | One executed |

## References

60. Caes. B. G. I. 12. Flor. IV. 2. 3

61. Caes. B. C. I. 13

62. Caes. B. C. I. 15

63. Caes. B. C. I. 18. 4

64. Flor. IV. 2. 3; Vell. Pat. II. 50; Caes. B. C. I. 20. 24 cf. 32. 8; App. II.

65. Caes. B. C. I. 24. 3

66. Caes. B. C. I. 78. 2

67. Caes. B. C. I. 74-78; App. II. 43 cf. Caes. B. C. I. 85

68. Caes. B. C. II. 20. 4

69. Dio 41. 26 ff.; Suet. Jul. 69; Front. Strat. IV. 5. 2; cf. Dio 41. 31. 1; 35.5
    App. II. 47; Dig. 49. 16. 3. 19

70. Caes. B. C. II. 27. 1

71. Caes. B. C. III. 13. 2; Dio 41. 48. 1; App. B. C. II. 55

72. Caes. B. C. III. 59-61

73. Caes. B. C. III. 60. 5

74. App. B. C. II. 61-63 cf. Caes. B. C. III. 74

75. Flor. IV. 2. 52; Caes. B. C. III. 104. 3

76. Bell. Alex. 48. 2-3; 52. 5; 53. 4; 56. 4; 57. 1; 57. 5; Dio 43. 29. 1

77. Dio 42. 52; Bell. Afr. 19. 3; Suet. Jul. 70; App. B. C. II. 92-94

78. Dio 43. 24

| Case | B.C. | Commander | Offenders | Offense | Circumstances | Outcome |
|------|------|-----------|-----------|---------|---------------|---------|
| 79. | 46 | Trebonius and Caesarian commanders | Spanish army | Revolt | Civil war | Escape to enemy |
| 80. | 46 | Cn. Pompey | Allobroges | Desertion | Civil war | No mention |
| 81. | 46 | ? | Afranius' men | Desertion | Civil war | No mention |
| 82. | 46 | Scipio | Numidians and Gaetulians | Desertion on four different occasion | Civil war against Caesar | No punishment |
| 83. | 46 | Caesar | Guards | Negligence | Caesar's guards at Thapsus allow enemy to capture two ships | Dishonorable discharge with severe threat |
| 84. | 46 | Caesar | Two military tribunes and three centurions | Insubordination and seditious tendency | A military tribune puts own interests above state's in transporting troops from Sicily to Africa | Dishonorable discharge |
| 85. | 46 | Caesar | Cavalry and light armed soldiers | Disorderliness | Fight losing battle without orders against Scipio's army | No cognizance of matter taken |
| 86. | 46 | Caesar | Army | Disorderliness | Eager for battle, Caesar's troops could not be restrained at Thapsus | No cognizance take |
| 87. | 45 | Cn. Pompey | Army | Desertions on six different occasions | Civil war against Caesar | No punishment possible |
| 88. | 44 | Antony | Roman soldiers | Mutiny | Civil war | Leaders of mutiny killed |
| 89. | 44 | Antony | Roman soldiers | Riot | Civil war | Change officers |
| 90. | 44 | Antony | Two legions | Desertion | Civil war | No mention |
| 91. | 44 | D. Brutus | Troops | Desertion | Accounts differ | Brutus slain |
| 92. | 42 | M. Brutus | Troops | Mutiny | Civil war | The worst offenders slain |
| 93. | 42 | Cassius | Troops | Lax and stubborn; some desert | Civil war | No mention |
| 94. | 39 | Calvinus | Two centuries | Cowardice | Lieutenant and men ambushed | Decimation |
| 95. | 36 | Ocatavian | Army | Seditious | Awaiting orders | Older ones dismissed |

24

## References

79. Dio 43. 29; *Bell. Hisp.* 7. 5; 12. 2

80. Dio 43. 29; Caes. *B. C.* I. 74 ff.

81. Dio 43. 29; Caes. *B. C.* 74 ff.

82. *Bell. Afr.* 32. 3; 35. 4-5-6; 55. 1; 56. 3; Dio 43. 4. 2

83. *Bell. Afr.* 44-46; Dio 43. 6. 3

84. *Bell. Afr.* 54

85. *Bell. Afr.* 61. 3-5

86. *Bell. Afr.* 82. 2-4; 85. 9

87. *Bell. Hisp.* 2. 2; 16. 4; 18. 3; 18. 6; 18. 9; 20. 2; 20. 4; 21. 1; 26. 2

88. App. *B. C.* III. 43; 56; Dio 45. 13; Vell. Pat, II. 61; Tac. *Ann.* I. 10

89. App. *B. C.* III. 44; Dio 45. 13. 3; 45. 38; Vell. Pat. II. 61

90. App. *B. C.* III. 45; Dio 45. 13; 45. 38; Vell. Pat. II. 61

91. App. *B. C.* III. 97; Vell. Pat. II. 64

92. App. *B. C.* 79; Dio 47. 23; Plut. *Brut.* 26; Vell. Pat. II. 69

93. Plut. *Brut.* 39

94. Dio 48. 42; Vell. Pat. II. 78. 3

95. Vell. Pat. II. 81; Dio 49. 13; App. *B. C.* V. 128-129

| Case | B.C. | Commander | Offenders | Offense | Circumstances | Outcome |
|---|---|---|---|---|---|---|
| 96. | 36 | Antony | Army | Cowardice | Unsuccessful siege | Some decimated; some placed on barley ration |
| 97. | 36 | Lepidus | 20 legions | Desertion | Civil war | No punishment |
| 98. | 35 | Octavian | Re-enlisted | Stubborn | Preparations against Celtic and Illyrian tribes | Some punished; some discharged |
| 99. | 34 | Octavian | Roman army | Cowardice | Difficult siege | Decimation and rations cut |
| 100. | 31 | Antony | Army, allied king and C. Domitius | Desertion | Civil war | No punishment |
| 101. | ? | Aquilius | Some centuries | Cowardice | ? | Three of each century executed |
| 102. | ? | Sulla | Some cohorts and centuries | Cowardice | ? | Made stand with helmets on and ungirdled at head quarters |

# References

96. Dio 49. 26. 3; 50. 27. 5; 48. 26. 3; Plut. *Ant*. 39; Front. *Strat*. IV. 1. 37

97. App. *B. C.* V. 123-126; Dio 49. 12; Vell. Pat. II. 80

98. Dio 49. 34. 3 ff. cf. *Dig*. 49. 16. 3. 21

99. Dio 49. 3S; App. X. 26

100. Vell. Pat. II. 84

101. Front. *Strat*. IV. 1. 36

102. Front. *Strat*. IV. 1. 27

# II.
# GENERAL CONCLUSIONS BASED ON TOTAL DATA REGARDING PUNISHABLE MILITARY OFFENSES

The total number of cases in which we have evidence that an offense against the military oath was committed preceding the empire is 193. Of these 102 were punished or reprimanded and 91 were unpunished or punishment is not reported. That is, beyond all doubt 53 per cent were punished. Now if we arrive at the real attitude towards punishing military offense, we must make several allowances. Cases of mutiny which reached the magnitude of revolution, and which succeeded in conjunction with the people must be deducted. Of these there were 4: the revolt from the Tarquins, the first secession to the Sacred Mount, and the second secession to the Sacred Mount involving two armies. We must further deduct all cases in which there was no power to punish the offender. This happened in the mutiny of Gnaeus Scipio's crew in 260 when the mutineers escaped to the enemy; in 88 when officers of the losing faction were killed; in 84 when Cinna, a general of the losing faction, was killed; in 78 in the case of Brutus, likewise a general of the losing faction; in 72 when Sertorius was killed; in 55 when the insolent remnants of Crassus' army were killed by the Parthians. The same is true in civil war when desertion took place to the winning side,—forty cases in all. The sum of these 3 types of cases is 50. Disregarding them we should find 71.3 per cent of offenses punished. Now there are 7 additional cases of desertion to the enemy not in time of civil war. Inasmuch as failure to regain these deserters or lack of definite knowledge on the part of the authors must account for silence as to their punishment, to get at the Roman attitude towards punishment, these cases must be deducted. For no one who reads of the extremely cruel punishments of deserters to the enemy when captured, could argue that any would ever have been pardoned.[3] There are 4 additional incidents called desertion by some authors, which are accounted for in other ways by other writers. We should have left only 30 cases in which offenders were not punished even if we consider silence on the part of the

---

[3] Cf. Dig. -19.16.3.11; 49.16.5.1-4 ; also the Cases, The Punic Wars Period, nos. 15, 17, 21, 30, 34, 46 ; The Late Republican Period nos. 1, 5, 13, and 58.

authors certain proof of impunity. 30 cases out of 132, or 22.7 per cent represents the proportion of offenses that one could readily argue escaped punishment.

These offenses include mutiny, individual insubordination, disorderliness, plundering, neglect of duty, and desertion of post. Strife between the patricians and plebeians, extenuating circumstances such as dangerous crises or disaster after battle, the generosity of some commanders and the weakness of others account for failure to exact punishment of offenders in the Roman army.

# 1. MUTINY

Of 30 cases of mutiny altogether, 13 were punished or reprimanded and 17 were not, or the authors have failed to record punishment. Of the latter 8 could net have been punished for the reasons mentioned previously. Therefore 13 out of 22, or 59 per cent, were punished when punishment was possible. Probable explanations for omission of punishment of these 9 mutinies with their dates are as follows: in 455, party strife of patricians and plebeians; in 342, oppression of debt; in 218, extenuating circumstances; in 140, fault of the commander; in 89, fault of the commander; in 89, ringleader turned over to civil law which allowed miscarriage of justice; in 87, fault of commander; in 86, weakness of commander; these troops were later reformed; in 36, justice of the cause and generosity of the commander. The operation of justice disposed of at least 5 cases. As to the other 4, we shall have to admit laxness on the part of the Romans if, as seems to be the fact, punishment was not inflicted.

The instances of mutiny punished are distributed as follows: 1 in the Early Period, 4 in the Punic Wars, and 8 in the Late Republican Period. The percentage of cases of mutiny punished is highest for the Punic Wars period. This seems to uphold the general statements of the ancients in regard to discipline, for they drew largely upon this period for examples of sternness.

Let us examine and compare the punishments themselves with the dates: in 413, a few put to death by civil law; in 256, the ringleader threatened with death; in 206, 35 ringleaders beheaded, all severely reprimanded and compelled to renew oath;[4] in 205, those at fault beaten or died in prison; in 199, reprimanded and promised adjustment of complaint; in 88, rebuke by general of opposing faction even; in 76, degradation and disbandment of the legion;[5] in 58, rebuke; in 49, leaders put to death and oth-

---

[4] Cf. Dig. 49.16.3.19.
[5] Cf. Dig. 49.16.3.20.

ers dismissed; in 48, war waged upon mutineers; in 47, some dismissed,[6] others exposed to dangerous service; in 44, leaders decimated; in 42, the worst put to death. The death sentence of the leaders of serious mutinies was resorted to in all periods. A list of names of commanders employing it is interesting. It is comprised of these: Scipio Africanus, Julius Caesar, Mark Antony, and Marcus Brutus.

## 2. INSUBORDINATION OF INDIVIDUALS

There are very few pronounced instances of insubordinate individuals mentioned by the authors. I have noted 8 in all, 6 punished and 2 unpunished. The tendency of men as a rule to generalize from one example is illustrated in the case of Lucius Papirius Cursor, the dictator, against Quintus Fabius, his master of horse. The incident in which the dictator apparently insisted upon the death of his master of horse for engaging in battle against orders, though with the greatest success, when all classes, soldiers, senators, tribunes, and plebeians would have exonerated him, seems to have lingered in the minds of generations[7] and to have impressed itself as a proof of extremely strict discipline of the early days. Yet, after the dictator had convinced all that the principles of military discipline were at stake, he pardoned Fabius. Other punishments besides death for insubordination were exile and dishonorable discharge. Of these 2 the first seems to us severe and, as it was infected in 180, we have another proof of the sternness of the period of the Punic Wars.

## 3. DISORDERLINESS

In this category there fall 22 cases, 12 punished and 10 unpunished, or 54.5 per cent punished. The Early Period has a high percentage of unpunished cases due primarily to the antipathy of the plebeians towards the patricians. On the other hand, 66 per cent of punishable cases in the Late Republican Period were punished. In the Punic Wars Period the majority of cases received punishment. These punishments with their specific offenses and dates are as follows: in 471, intentional unruliness, guilty centurions and standard bearers scourged and beheaded, private soldiers decimated; in 252, refused to work, branded by censors and pay denied by vote of senate and people; in 212, insubordination and insolence, assignment to indefinite, undesirable service; in 177, disobedience and mockery, discharge; in 86, rioting, punished (no details mentioned) ; in 81, lack of

---

[6] Cf. Dig. 49.16.3.21.
[7] Cf. Din. 49.16.3.15.

restraint, punished; in 74, lawlessness and stubbornness, punished; in 72, rebellious spirit displayed, some put to death, some punished or threatened and some rewarded; in 52, rashness, reprimanded; in 46, rioting, one executed as an example ; in 44, rioting, officers changed; in 35, stubbornness, some punished, some dishonorably discharged. In the first case in 471 when the troops of Appius Claudius purposely disobeyed and threw away their standards they unintentionally risked punishment for greater offenses, those of loss of standards and desertion for which the laws fixed the death penalty.[8] With the exception of 2 or 3 of the other cases we can hardly say that the punishments were severe.

## 4. LAXNESS

Laxness of the Roman armies was tolerated most in the Early period although the severest punishments were also inflicted in that period. Out of a total of 19 cases, 73.6 per cent of instances of laxness was punished or reformed with sternness. For the Punic Wars period the percentage is even higher. The specific offenses, punishments and their dates are as follows: in 418, standard bearer lagging in battle, slain by general's own hand; in 390, asleep on duty, hurled from the cliff of the Capitolium;[9] in 252, negligence, beaten and rank reduced; in 218, negligence, punished; in 195, lagging, struck with weapon; in 195/194 negligence, punished; in 176, allowing the commander to be killed, deprived of pay and credit for the campaign; in 132, negligence, dishonorable discharge; in 109, indulgence and negligence, severely punished; in 46, negligence, dishonorable discharge and severe threat. In 169 the lax army operating against Perses was reformed by Aemilius Paulus. In 147 the lax army before Carthage and in 134 that at Numantia was sternly reformed by Scipio Aemilianus. The types of punishment above mentioned would justify the word "strict" as descriptive of them.

## 5. CRIMINALITY

Crime was punished in 10 cases out of 11 mentioned. At the capture of Phocaea, plundering against orders is mentioned without any record of punishment. The specific offenses, their dates and punishments are as follows: in 449, murder, death, or exile under civil law;[10] in 343, criminal plot, secret prevention by discharge; in 280/271, murder, flogged and put

---

[8] Cf. p. 41 and Cf. Dig. 49.16.3.22.
[9] Cf. Dig. 49.16.3.6.;— 10.1.
[10] Cf. Dig. 49.16.4.5.

to death ; in 205, theft from temple, twofold restoration under threat of death;9 in 204, murder, death of some drawn by lot; in 203, plot to burn camp, put to death;[11] in 192/185, disgraceful murder by general, expulsion from the senate by the Censor; in 88, plunder, punished ; in 87, plunder and murder, put to death; in 76, disrespect to women, put to death. It will be seen that the death penalty generally followed crime at all periods.

# 6. DESERTION

Desertion from the Roman armies is the hardest of all offenses to deal with accurately. We must keep in mind that soliciting desertion was one of the chief methods of warfare of the ancients. On the other hand the laws of the Romans were very strict in regard to it. Desertion as defined by Appian might apply to any soldier who went beyond hearing distance of the bugle. Dionysius of Halicarnassus states that the Roman law gave power to the generals to put to death without a trial all who were disobedient, or deserted their en signs.[12] So probability from these two standpoints always leaves one in doubt in a given case. Another difficulty arises in the use of the various words of the original texts referring to the subject. For example Dionysius evidently uses the same word (αὐτολεῖν) to refer to those violating the military oath, to slaves accompanying the army, to noncombatant citizens of a town, and even to slaves not engaged in warfare. Furthermore the writers do not distinguish various kinds of desertion, but with justice to the soldiers it seems necessary to distinguish 3 degrees of offense; desertion to the enemy, leaving the ensigns only, and running in battle without orders to retreat.

In the face of these and other difficulties I have found what I believe to be the facts as follows: The chances of safety for the deserter were slightly in his favor if we include cases of desertion to the enemy in time of civil war. For the deserter had to be caught before he was punished. Out of a total of 100 cases possibly 53, i.e. 53 per cent, were unpunished. But of these 40 occurred in the civil wars of the late period in which the soldier is hardly to be blamed for choosing the winning side and therefore they have little to do with military discipline. Indeed in some cases as the designs of leaders changed, desertion occurred as a duty to country.[13] If we deduct these forty cases we shall see that desertion was dangerous for the soldier of the Roman army since it was punished in 78 per cent of cases. Recovery and punishment of deserters to a foreign enemy is mentioned in 68 per

---

[11] Cf. Dig. 49.16.5.1.
[12] V. p. 40 ; cf. p. 41.
[13] Cf. Case no. 20 of the Late Republican Period.

cent of the cases. That Roman citizens deserted in violation of the military oath would be hard to prove for the Early period. There are instances in the other two periods. The punishments and dates of desertions in these periods are interesting: in 214, Romans flogged and thrown from the Tarpeian Rock; in 214, allies, put to death; in 211, allied deserters, hands cut off; in 208, Latin speaking deserters, put to death by allied city; in 201, Latin deserters beheaded, Roman crucified; in 194, Roman or allied, put to death; in 171 and 168, allies, thrown under elephants to be trampled to death ; in 146, Roman deserters burned themselves in preference to capture, allied deserters thrown to beasts in gladiatorial shows;[14] in 138, possibly Roman, flogged and sold at auction—in one case for a sesterce; in 108, allies, hands cut off or half buried, struck with spears and burned while still breathing; in 90, Numidians discharged for tendency to desert ; in 85, Romans or allies, punished; in 74, Romans inclined to desert, punished; in 49, Romans inclined to desert, punished with cruelty. By the expression "inclined to desert," reference is made to cases in which comrades of deserters were punished on the ground that they intended to desert later. After a review of this list of punishments we are surely justified in saying the Romans were strict on deserters to a foreign enemy. And it is improbable that they ever let such recaptured deserters go unpunished.

Leaving the standards or one's post was punished in 7 cases, out of a possible 11. The unpunished cases, all, are enshrouded in some doubt. In 67, Lucullus' army deserted, but some accounts state that it was after hearing that their discharge had been decreed at Rome. In 55, Ignatius and his horsemen left Crassus' army after its disaster and were styled deserters, but in doing so rendered service to the unfortunate army. In 48, Pompey was slain by a deserter from his own army, according to Florus. Caesar states he had been a centurion under Pompey in the war with the Pirates. In 44, Decimus Brutus lost the most of his troops by desertion because of hardships in his attempt to join forces with his brother, Marcus. These, especially the veterans, joined the enemy only for self-preservation.

The punishments for desertion of post or the ensigns were severe. In Tullus Hostilius' reign Mettius Fufetius and his Alban subjects, for desertion of post with intent to join the winning side, were punished as follows: Mettius was torn asunder by being tied to chariots driven in opposite directions; his accomplices were put to death when found guilty; the common soldiers were moved to Rome with the destruction of their town. In 431, Postumius was reported to have put to death his son for deserting his post to fight with the enemy against orders, though successful. Livy did

---

[14] Cf. Dig. 49.16.4.1.

not believe the report, In 396 deserters from camp were punished. In 340, Manlius put to death his own son for deserting his post to fight a duel, though he brought back victory.[15] This gained him the title "Imperiosus" and probably did more to impress the idea of stern discipline of the early republic on the minds of succeeding generations than any other one event. In 180, a legion leaving service by unauthorized discharge when brought back received half pay. If any did not return they were subject to confiscation of goods and being sold into slavery. In 145/144 Celtiberi deserting Roman garrisons in Spain were punished by cutting off their hands. In 54, Caesar had Dumnorix put to death for leading away his cavalry from service in the Roman army with treacherous intent. This was the second case of his disloyalty.

Running in battle or cowardice was punished almost without exception at all times.[16] In 393, an army fled from fear because of an uncertain report of the defeat of comrades in the vicinity. Punishment is not mentioned. In 102, Catulus ran to the front of his fleeing army and pretended to have authorized the flight as a stratagem to regain control. He led them back to victory. In 23 other cases punishment was dealt out. 8 of these fell in the Early period with penalties as follows: ordered to face enemy or to be killed in 2 cases; rebuke, loss of part in spoils and general reduced in rank; severe rebuke; those chosen by lot slain; made camp outside the rampart without tents ; degradation ; winter in tents. In the Punic Wars Period 5 cases were punished as follows: camp outside of rampart; indefinite undesirable service with barley for rations for 7 years; always stand while eating as long as in the army; reprimanded, barley as rations, and standing in the praetorium without belts and withdrawn swords for a time; ordered to return to the fight or to be killed. In the Late Republican Period 10 cases were punished as follows: assignment to a dangerous exploit; degradation; put to death (the offense was combined with a suspicion of disloyalty); chastisement and work; decimation; degradation of leaders (the army itself asked to be decimated out of shame); decimation; some decimated and some given barley; decimation and rations cut; some made to stand at headquarters with helmets on and ungirdled. In one case of uncertain date 3 of each century were put to death. These punishments on the whole were severe.

It will be seen that the Late Republican period employed the severest punishments for the offense under consideration. This is due to the fact that several of the commanders felt no accountability to the people as the

---

[15] Cf. Dig. 49.16.3.15;— 3.22.
[16] Cf. Dig. 49.16.6.3.

early consuls did. In 471, when Appius Claudius employed decimation for the same offense committed in the spirit of disobedience, he did so to his own ruin the next year. For he was brought to trial and committed suicide when he saw he would be condemned by the people. 400 years later Crassus employed decimation in the war with Spartacus and came off honored by all. That there must have been other cases of decimation in the meantime is indicated by Polybius' explanation of the theory of its employment as if it were a principle of Roman discipline.[17] He praises the Romans that they had found a method of punishment which in effect was severe, but was free from the offensiveness of severity. For instead of putting to death all the guilty for a capital offense they put to death every tenth man chosen by lot. In several instances between the 2 dates mentioned, a smaller proportion were put to death. Small parts of their armies were decimated by Caesar, by Calvinus, a general of Octavian, by Octavian himself, and by Antony. More cases of decimation are mentioned from 71-34 B.C. than in all the rest of Roman history down to the empire.

## 7. MISCELLANEOUS CASES

Beating with rods,[18] and the mark of disgrace[19] were employed in 3 cases, 2 in the first Punic War and 1 in the last century of the republic for offenses not mentioned.

## 8. CONCLUSIONS

It will be seen from the preceding discussion that in spite of the praise of the early Romans for strict discipline by the writers of the Augustan age, the armies of the late republic were as strictly or more strictly punished. It is a common failing of all to underestimate the virtues of their own age in comparison with former ages. Yet it should not surprise us to find that punishments were as strictly inflicted in the late republic as in the earlier periods. The Romans as a nation had not even at the close of the republic made their army as perfect an instrument for conquest and domination as it later became. The citizen soldier of the republic could hardly be expected to sink his individuality so completely in mass action, to become an automaton in the hands of his commander, a mere cog in a perfect military machine, so completely as did the professional soldier of Caesar's day and of the empire.

---

[17] Polyb. VI. 38.
[18] Cf. Dig. 49.16.3.5:— 3.16;— 14.1.
[19] CI. Dig. 49.16.3.5;—3.14;—3.20.

Since the death penalty was assessed in 40 cases out of 102 where the punishment is mentioned, it is clear that punishment in the Roman army was severe in comparison with that in modern armies. The instances of the infliction of the death penalty are distributed almost equally among the 3 periods. From this viewpoint military discipline did not suffer a decline before the establishment of the empire. The cruel practice of scourging those to be put to death went out of use before the end of the third century B.C., if the historians have given us all the facts. The dates of such incidents were 672, 471, 271, and 214. Scourging[20] by itself or accompanied by light additional punishment lasted till later as the following dates indicate: 252, 249, 205, 138, and 86. It is, of course, likely that this punishment was employed in some instances in which the authors do not give the specific form of punishment. Cutting off of the hands of allied deserters was practiced mostly, if not exclusively, during little more than 1 century. There was 1 such case in 211, another in 145, and another in 108. This group of facts indicates stringency during or near the period of the Punic Wars especially. The last century before our era seems to have attained to greater mercy in punishments along with advanced culture.

---

[20] Cf. note 16.

# III.

# THE NATURE OF MILITARY DISCIPLINE OF THE ROMANS AS INDICATED BY GENERAL STATEMENTS OF THE SOURCES

## 1. THE EARLY PERIOD

Restraint of the natural impulses of soldiers who were not delinquent in military service is indicated in passages giving the tradition of the Early period with dates as follows: 753/717, Romulus taught his farmer-soldiers collected on market days for drill not to yield to others in war either from toils or advantages (Dion. Hal. *Antiq. Rom.* II. 28.3); 715, Numa upon coming to the throne in Rome decided that the people, made fierce by wars, whom fear of an enemy and military discipline had restrained, needed to be inspired by the fear of the gods (Liv. I. 19.4) ; 578/534, Servius Tullius chose as captains those most capable in things relating to war and saw to it that the company of each was very obedient to commands (Dion. Hal. *Antiq. Rom.* IV. 17.4); 494, when the people agitated secession, the senate ordered the consuls not to disband the legions and none of the soldiers, bound by their military oaths, ventured to desert their ensigns (Dion. Hal. *Antiq. Rom.* VI. 45.1); 460, the military oath made an efficient army in spite of civjl discord (Dion. Hal. *Antiq. Rom.* - X. 16.1; Liv. III. 18. 7-8); 394, the soldiers, though angered at Camillus because he turned the spoils into the public treasury, nevertheless were subdued by his sternness of command (Liv. V. 26.8); 385, Camillus ordered his men to await the attack of the Volscians and their allies in a stationary line and they obeyed (Liv. VI. 12.8-11); 357, the tribunes of the people did not allow a precedent of calling an assembly of the people apart from the regular place to stand, for a consul could get any measure he wished passed if his soldiers, bound to him by military oath, were allowed to vote it (Liv. VII. 16.7-8); 275, the Romans adopted surveying of the camp from Pyrrhus, which brought a whole army within one rampart and assigned to each body of troops a definite part of the camp. This placed them under the constraint of system (Front. *Strat.* IV. 1.14; Liv. 35.14; Plut. *Pyrrh.* 16).

Measures imposing hardships upon the soldiers indicate sternness of command. In 616/578, Servius Tullius in a battle in which king Tarquin fought the Sabines seized a standard and threw it among the enemy (Front. *Strat*. II. 8.1; cf. Dion Hal. *Antiq. Rom*. 3.65). In 488, the consul Aquilius seized standards of indifferent cohorts and threw them among the enemy that the dread of punishment ordained by the laws for those losing their standards might compel them to fight valiantly (Dion. Hal. *Antiq. Rom*. VIII. 65.5) to recover them. Camillus' aggressiveness is illustrated again in 486 (Liv. VI. 8.3; Front. *Strat*. II. 8.4) when he seized a standard bearer and marched him to the front, at length commanding him to throw the standard among the enemy. Servilius, consul in 476, is represented as defending himself against charges of cruelty of command the following year by citing how generals had thrown ensigns among the enemy, had burned their tents and provisions to compel the soldiers to fight for sustenance, and had burned bridges to prevent retreat without being called to account (Dion. Hal. *Antiq. Rom*. IX. 31.3). In 446, Furius Agrippa in battle with the Hernici and Aequi, threw the standard among the enemy (Liv. III. 70.2-11). T. Quinctius Capitolinus threw a standard among the enemy while encountering the Falisci in 431, (Front. *Strat*. II. 8.3; aliter Liv. IV. 26-29). The sternness of the senate is illustrated by their decree, in 279, (Plut. *Pyrrh*. 20.5; App. III. 10.5) that Roman prisoners released by Pyrrhus for the celebration of a festival should be put to death if they failed to return to him.

The tradition that the military laws were strict is indicated by Dionysius in these passages referring to the early period: in 488, punishment for loss of ensigns (Dion. Hal. *Antiq. Rom*. VIII. 65.5: X. 36) ; in 460, Lucius Quinctius, consul suffectus, quieted disturbances of the people by reminding them of their military oaths to the former consuls and by threatening to use all the rigor of the laws against them (Dion. Hal. *Antiq. Rom*. X. 18); the punishment for quitting post was death, according to the laws (Dion. Hal. *Antiq. Rom*. VIII. 79). that the death penalty was not prevented in the army by the Valerian law (Plut. Pop. 10.5), is indicated by the fact that Coriolanus had the axes left out of the fasces when he went to salute his mother. The removal of the axes from the fasces of the general as a mark of reverence toward anyone became a custom that was continued by the Romans down to the time of Augustus (Dion. Hal. *Antiq. Rom*. VIII. 44.3). the use of the axes in the army is again indicated when the Decemvirs in 450 used the fasces including the axes in the city, which was customary only on military expeditions and. journeys away from the city (Dion. Hal. *Antiq. Rom*. X. 59.5).

The early Romans as well as those of later centuries recognized an art of generalship. By various means the men themselves were led to uphold bravery and compliance with commands. Romulus started the practice of dividing spoils with the army that the men might engage willingly in expeditions (Dion. Hal. *Antiq. Rom.* II, 28). In 495, Publius Servilius used the division of the spoils from the Volscians to his own advantage and that of the state (Dion. Hal. *Antiq. Rom.* VI. 29.4). Marcus Valerius Corvus inspired his troops to fight against the Sabines "with eyes like fire" in 343 chiefly by participating in the soldiers' contests of strength and swiftness like a common soldier (Liv. VII. 33).

The results sometimes mentioned by the historians could not have been attained except by discipline, both of training inculcated by commanders, and of voluntary compliances on the part of the men. In Romulus' reign after a raid of the Veientes into Roman territory, the Roman king led his troops across the Tiber and encountered the enemy in the open field. There, without the aid of any strategy, merely by the strength of his veteran army Romulus routed the enemy and pursued them to their walls (Liv. I. 15.4). The proverbial Pyrrhic victory after which the invading king found all the fallen Romans with wounds in front argues strongly that discipline among the early Romans was strictly kept.

There are, however, a few instances in which weak discipline must be admitted. Enmity between the patricians and plebeians accounts for an example in 495 (Dion. Hal. *Antiq. Rom.* VI. 29), another in 483 (Dion. Hal. *Antiq. Rom.* VIII. 89.3), and still another in 480 (Dion. Hal. *Antiq. Rom.* IX. 7-10; Liv. II. 44; 45-47; Front. *Strat.* I. 11.1). In this last case, the army finally aroused itself and showed great bravery. Eagerness in battle was sometimes detrimental to good order as in 495 (Dion. Hal. *Antiq. Rom.* 31.3) and in 435 (Liv. IV. 18). Strife between the commanders in 418 did harm to the morale of the soldiers. In regard to the death of Q. Aulius Cerretanus in 315, the authors differ. Diodorus (XIX. 72.7-8) attributed his death to the cowardice of his men, but Livy (IX. 22.4-10) puts whatever blame there was on Aulius himself.

Mention of desertion in the early history of the Romans seems to refer to slaves or non-combatants. When the Sabines besieged Rome, a man sent by Tarpeia to Romulus with information deserted[21] to the Sabines, according to Piso, whom Dionysius considered the most reliable of his sources. If we do not even regard the whole story as a legend, we should not expect a soldier to take orders from a mere girl. Neither would he have been likely to expect a greater reward from the Sabine than the Roman

---

[21] Dion. Hal. Antiq. Rom. II. 39.1.

king unless he had been a slave and hoped to gain his freedom. Tarquinius Pricus, 616/578, took cities of the Latins and ordered them to deliver up the deserters[22] and captives. These deserters could have been camp followers. Deserters[23] fighting with the exiles against the Romans at the battle of Lake Regillus, in 499, were not necessarily those who had broken a military oath. From Dionysius' use of the word αὐτομολεῖν we should be inclined to think he had in mind others besides soldiers. He indicates that slaves and the rabble deserted[24] to Porsena when Rome was besieged by him. The circumstances described in Dionysius VI. 21.2, VIII. 22.1, and VIII. 86.3 permit the same interpretation of αὐτόμολος. Of the foraging incidents or statements of facts 60 per cent indicate strictness of Roman military discipline in the Early period. In addition 6 per cent can be taken as argument that good discipline, at least, existed. A little more than 19 percent of the incidents refer to desertion of non-combatants or incidents that cannot indicate weak discipline when all the references are assembled, although an isolated passage, especially in English translation, would be so understood. Some over 14 per cent of the references are to cases of weak discipline due to enmity between patricians and plebeians, rivalry of commanders, or too much eagerness of the soldiers for battle. General statements are more abundant in the ancient writers indicating strictness in the Early period than they are referring to the later centuries.

---

[22] Dion. Hal. Antiq. Rom. III. 64.2.

[23] Dion. Hal. Antiq. Rom. VI. 5.4.

[24] Dion. Hal. Antiq. Rom. VI. 2.2.

# 2. THE PUNIC WARS PERIOD

The restraint that many of the great Roman generals showed in their own lives is a good indication that their soldiers were required to practice restraint. Of 7 Roman generals named by Frontinus (*Strat.* IV. 3.1-4, 9, 12, 15) as examples of continence, the majority commanded during this period and all of them very near it. The sternness of Cato, the Censor, is well known and materially helps to bring up the general average of severity during this period. He handed down, most likely in his work on military discipline,[25] knowledge of a rigid punishment of theft in the army, a subject on which most of the authors were silent. The right hand of those caught in theft among fellow soldiers was sometimes cut off. A lighter punishment was given for that offense by exposing the culprit at headquarters bleeding (Front. *Strat.* IV. 1.16 ; Gell. X. 8.1) . That an irregularity was likely to be punished during this period, is indicated by a mishap to Marcus Cato, son of the Censor. Fearing ignominy for losing his sword when his horse fell in battle (168), he incurred great danger to recover it. (Front. *Strat.* IV. 5.17; Val. Max. III. 2.16; Justin. 33.2; Plut. *Aem.* 21.)

The most famous discourse on the strictness of camp discipline is that of Polybius VI. 37-38,[26] which indicates that the fear of punishments produced faultless attention to duty, especially in the night watches. It carries weight from the prestige of the author, who was describing what he had an opportunity to see with his own eyes. His statements are duplicated in a general way by others. Vegetius speaks of daily attention to strictness of discipline by the prefect of the legion (Mil. II. 9). And Vegetius certainly maintains[27] that the earlier Romans disciplined more strictly than those of his day. Valerius Maximus also refers to sharp observation of camp discipline and military theory (II. 8 intro.; II. 9 intro.). To the former he attributes the extensive conquests and power of Rome. Polybius (XXX. 6) places the practical accomplishment of Rome's control of the world in 167 with the fall of King Perses. The two statements together, if wholly true, are conclusive proof of strict discipline for the period under discussion.

Although Greek luxury was supposed to make its advent among the Romans from the fall of Syracuse in 212 (Liv. XXV. 40), yet we learn in one marked example, that of P. Scipio, that its adoption did not necessarily operate against discipline. At the instigation of Fabius Maximus, Scip-

---

[25] Cell. VI. 4.5. ; Veg. Res Mil. I. 15.

[26] Running a guantlet of cudgels {L. fustuarium) is referred to as punishment for faulty night watches, stealing, false witnessing, and injuring one's own body; decimation for desertion of the ranks because of cowardice is also mentioned.

[27] Veg. Mil. I. 21.

io's army was inspected by a committee, but was found to be in good discipline. (Liv. XXIX. 22.) Although his brother was convicted on a charge incurred in his command against Antiochus who attempted with some success to fight the Romans with luxury, the decision was admitted to have been given by a corrupt judge. That military success in difficult wars was a proof of stern discipline is shown in the case of Paulus, who counteracted the influence of Perses' wealth with which he had cleverly stood off the Romans by corrupting them, and again before Carthage when Scipio Aemilianus banished easy life from the camp.

As a disciplinary measure in 216 the military oath was expanded to include by requirement what had been added voluntarily in former times (Front. Strat. IV. 1.4; Liv. XXXII. 38.1-5; Polyb. VI. 21;-33; Gell. XVI. 4.2).

In 214, Pinarius, the stern commander of the garrison in Henna, is represented by Livy (24.37) as saying to the townsmen, who were scheming to bring about a revolt, that to depart from a garrison was a capital offense among the Romans.

There are occasional indications of judicious relaxation of discipline during the Punic wars. Fabius Maximus, in 216, was said to have admitted that a certain Marcian who was agitating desertion had not been fairly treated and to have made him honorable presents by which he won his unwavering loyalty. (Plut. *Fab.* 20; Val. Max. 7.3. 7; Aur. Vic. *Vir. Ill.* 43; Liv. XXVII. 15.) Like stories were told of Marcellus (Liv. XXVIII. 15-16; Plut. *Marc.* 10-11; Dio XX. 33). Some instances of weak discipline during the period are noted by the historians. In 182 sickness of a general caused a decline of morale in an army mentioned by Livy (XL. 1.4). Weak generals are attributed with allowing discipline to decline and cause delay of success against Antiochus, Perses, and the Carthaginians, as has been mentioned.

Aside from the authenticated cases of desertion already mentioned, there are some passages in authors that indicate possible additional cases though it cannot be proved that slaves are not referred to. Treaties and terms of peace mention deserters on the following occasions: at the end of the first Punic war (Zon. 8.17; App. V. 2; Polyb. I. 62); at the close of the first Illyrian war, in 228, (App. X. 2.7); when Flamininus made peace with the Macedonians, in 196, (Liv. XXXII. 33.3 ; cf. XXXII. 30.5 ; Eutr. IV. 2.2 ; App. IX. 9.3 ; Zon. IX. 16 fin.); terms of surrender of Abracia and Aetolia, in 189, (Liv. XXXVIII. 9.9; 11.4; Polyb. XXI. 30.3); likewise of Antiochus, in 188, (Liv. XXXVIII. 38.8; Polyb. 21.45; App. XI. 38-39; Flor. I. 24.18; Diod. XXIX. 10). Two passages of Livy referring to 216 B.C. indicate opposite conclusions. From Livy XXIII. 12 fin. we should conclude that up to that time not a man of the thirty-five tribes had deserted in the Second Punic War. But in Livy XXIII. fin. we read of those slipping away without furloughs.

The foregoing passages when summed up unmistakably point to rigid discipline of Romans in the armies in the Punic War times, but to considerable more leniency towards allies. For the deserters mentioned, if not slaves, were probably allies in view of Vegetius' statement that allies were held under less rigid discipline than Romans (Mil. II. 3).

# 3. THE LATE REPUBLICAN PERIOD

Aggressive disciplining of armies in the late Roman republic is illustrated in numerous passages. Scipio at Numantia, in 134, has been mentioned (cf. Front. *Strat*. IV. 1.1; App. VI. 84). Marcus Scaurus' army in 115 left the fruit of an apple tree at the edge of its camp untouched (Front. *Strat*. IV. 3.13). The same general forbade his son, who had engaged in the retreat of Catulus before the Cimbri, in 102, to come into his presence, whereupon the son committed suicide out of remorse (Front. *Strat*. IV. 1.13; Val. V. 84). Quintus Metellus, in 109/102, though hindered by no law from keeping his son in his own tent with himself, made him serve in the ranks (Front. *Strat*. IV. 1.11); Publius Rutilius, in 105, the same (Front. Strat. IV. 1.12). The army of the same general was chosen by Caius Marius in preference to that of Metellus, though it was smaller, on the ground that Rutilius' men were of surer discipline (Front. *Strat*. IV. 2.2). Caius Marius is represented as taking part in all the hardships of the common soldier in his campaign against Jugurtha, in 107. Armed and ready for duty he compelled the soldiers to do as he himself did, but he drove the army by sense of shame rather than by punishment (Sall. *Jug*. 100.2-5). 4 years later he took command against the Cimbri and Teutons. He accustomed the soldiers to long marches and compelled each man to carry his own baggage on a forked stick of his own invention (Front. *Strat*. IV. 1.7; Plut. *Mar*. 13). Plutarch further describes his severe behavior and inflexibility in punishing, which the soldiers thought just and salutary after becoming accustomed to it. In authority, the same author says, he was fierce and untractable because more acquainted with camp than city discipline. Gnaeus Pompeius used strategy in summoning soldiers guilty of the slaying of the senate at Mediolanum by mingling with them innocent men. Thus he took away fear of obeying the summons from the guilty and had a guard to prevent mutiny. The implication is that the purpose of the summons was to punish the guilty (Front. *Strat*. I. 9.3). At the defeat of Tigranes by Lucullus in 69, the Roman soldiers passed by bracelets and necklaces on the read as they pursued the enemy because they had been forbidden to plunder by threats of punishment (App. XII. 85).

Caesar expected strict obedience and reminded his soldiers that the theory of military affairs, especially in naval actions, demanded that everything be done according to command and on time (*B. G*. IV. 23.5). Caesar's soldiers when entrapped by the enemy on account of disagreement between Sabinus and Cotta placed all hope of safety in courage (*B. G*. V. 34.2). Caesar's soldiers under Quintus Cicero showed their zeal for the safety of their commander in urging him to take rest (*B. G*. V. 40.7).

Later his soldiers complained against him for confining them to camp according to Caesar's orders. (*B. G.* VI. 36.1-2). The established theory and custom of the Roman army demanded that the maniples be kept with their standards (*B. G.* VI. 34.6; cf. *B. G.* VII. 45.8). At the siege of Massilia, in 49, by Trebonius, Caesar's lieutenant, the soldiers were restrained from taking the place by assault for fear they would kill the inhabitants of military age in accordance with a custom, not uncommon, of ancient warfare (Caes. *B. C.* II. 13.34).

Although Marcus Brutus inflicted the severest punishments on certain occasions, his colleague, Cassius, trained his men with more vigorous discipline (Front. *Strat.* IV. 2.2). After the battle of Actium, Octavian's army was held in restraint partly by their commanders and partly by the hope of participating in the spoils of Egypt (Dio LI. 3). After the event Scarpus did not even allow freedom of speech (Dio 41.5.6) in the army.

The fear of the law exerted its influence in the late republic as before.[28] In 55 when the soldiers of Crassus were opposed to his policy from fear of bad omens, they followed nevertheless from regard for the laws (Dio XL. 19). What these laws were can well be inferred from Appian's speech (VIII. 116) assigned to Scipio before Carthage, in which Scipio states to the soldiers that he had power to punish the disobedient with the utmost severity ; and that the laws required them to toil while danger lasted, postponing spoils till later.

To the credit of the soldiers it must be said that sometimes they showed more real character than their leaders. In 105 B.C. the soldiers of Servilius compelled him to do the right thing. Ordinarily the soldier of the earlier periods was a man of property, which was a pledge of his good behavior.

That good discipline generally existed is indicated by the generalship commonly employed in addition to measures of restraint. The greatest generals seldom had to resort to punishments. For example, Caesar nowhere mentions corporal punishment of his men during the Gallic Wars. However, he was an expert in the use of the arts of generalship. Among these are to be found the following: compliments passed on the soldiers (B. G. 1. 40-42); inspiration by his personal exploits (*B. G.* II. 25); gifts from the booty or other sources (*B. G.* VII. 11.9; 89.5; cf. Suet. *Jul.* 26; B. C. III. 53.5; *Bell. Alex.* 19.1; -42.3; *Bell. Afr.* 86.3; *Bell. Hisp.* 26.1); borrowing from the officers to pay the privates (Caes. B. C. I. 39.3; Suet. *Jul.* 68); promises (*B. G.* VII. 27); appeal to reason (*B. G.* VII. 19); skillful measures of various sorts (*B. G.* I. 52.1; II. 20.3; II. 33.1).

---

[28] Cf. p. 40.

A few passages implying weakness of discipline where soldiers were not considered guilty of offense are to be found. Caius Gracchus was supposed to have deserted the army when acting as quaestor in 124. Upon investigation it was found that he had served 2 years overtime (Plut. *Gracch.* 2). 2 years later he introduced a bill to prevent Latins from being scourged. It was probably annulled by Opimius (Plut. *Gracch.* 13). Marcus Drusus was said to have shown much leniency to his soldiers in 112 (Dio XXVI. 88). Even the greatness of Sulla did not prevent differences of his troops though he was near (Front. *Strat.* I. 9.2). Sertorius was mild in his punishments till the latter part of his life (Plut. *Ser.* 10.3).

Statements about desertion where insufficient knowledge is given to determine the circumstances indicate the possibility of a few cases not included in this study. The writers of the period use various expressions that are of broader application than our word desert with its specialized meaning.[29] Labienus was said to have deserted Caesar (Dio XLI. 51.1), but there is no proof that he was under obligation to serve Caesar in civil war. Slaves were said to desert (Dio XLVIII. 36. 3; cf. Dig. 49.16.3.10). In the Bellum Hispaniense, a woman is said to have deserted (transfugere 19.3). In the same work legions were enrolled from deserters (perfugis 34.2). This refers apparently to emancipated slaves and to refugees from other than Roman armies. When information is obtained frcm deserters (cf. Dio XLVIII. 40) nothing definite can be stated as to their former condition. Foreigners who engaged in war without obligation to do so, as in the case of Menas (Dio XLVIII. 45.7), apparently could change sides with impunity (Dio XLVIII. 54.7; XLIX. 1.4). The desertersin Sextus Pompeius' fleet at the battle of Mylae may or may not have broken a military oath when they joined him. At any rate changing sides in civil war was expected (Caes. *B. C.* II. 29.3) more than in a foreign war. One other feature of ancient desertion should be taken into account. Soldiers always lacked confidence in unlucky commanders (App. XII.108). A sort of religious superstition mitigated the feeling against those who left their generals after crushing defeat. Caesar recognized this principle in his exhortation to his soldiers before he met Ariovistus (*B. G.* I. 40.12). It was recognized in the case of Ignatius' desertion of Crassus. Caesar recognized the spell of fortune when he enlisted an officer named Scipio because his soldiers feared to go against a Scipio in Africa on account of Scipio Africanus' good fortune against Hannibal.

[29] Cf. p. 34.

# 4. FROM VEGETIUS AND THE DIGEST

Vegetius gives the impression that he had gleaned most of his discussions from the historians. That the picture he draws of the careful training of the Roman soldier was true for the republic is proved by Cicero's similar portrayal in the Tusculan Disputations (II. 16). Vegetius explicitly states that the discipline of his times was inferior to that of former times (Mil. 21). In another passage he states that the slow and negligent in drill were fed on barley till they mastered the whole drill (I. 13). He mentions the rear gate of the camp through which delinquents were led to punishment (I.23). In making the fortifications of the enemy, he says, the centurions were to inspect the work and those negligent were punished (I. 25). The system he described provided for the severest punishment. The classicum was the signal blown on the trumpet to announce an execution II. 22). Daily attention to strictness of discipline was the duty of the prefect of the legion (II. 9).

The Romans were a conservative people. It is likely that just as the strategems mentioned by Vegetius can nearly all be illustrated by events recorded in the history of the republic, so the laws collected by Justinian were framed from actual experiences, many of them drawn from republican history (Cf. Dig. 49.16.4). In the various writers of the Digest 49.16, eighteen offenses of soldiers are mentioned punishable by death. They are as follows: a scout remaining with the enemy (-3.4), desertion (-3.11; -5.1-3), losing or disposing of one's arms (-3.13), disobedience in war time (-3.15), going over the wall or rampart (-3.17), starting a mutiny (-3.19), refusing to protect an officer or deserting one's post (-3.22), a drafted man hiding from service (-4.2), murder (-4.5), laying hands on a superior or insult to a general (-6.1), leading flight when the example would influence others (-6.3), betraying plans to the enemy (-6.4 ; -7) , wounding a fellow soldier with a sword (-6.6), disabling self or attempting suicide without reasonable excuse (-6.7), leaving the night watch (-10.1), breaking the centurion's staff or striking him when being punished (-13.4), escaping guard house (-13.5), and disturbing the peace (-16.1) . Examples of nearly all of these offenses actually punished by death, as already given in the preceding chapters, strongly indicate the probability that the Justinian laws found their basis in republican as well as later history and give reliable information where other sources of information are lacking.

The list of punishments mentioned in addition provided restraint for every gradation of offense. They are: chastisement with lashes, exile, degradation, dishonorable discharge, change of service, fine, depriving of decorations of honor, and, for those not soldiers but affected by military laws, slavery and torture.

However, the Roman honestly attempted to mete out punishment according to justice as many of the laws indicate (v. *Dig.* 49.16.3.7; -3.10; -3.16; -4.13; -5.1; -5.5; -6.7-8; -14.1).

# Bibliography

Alton, E. H.
 The Roman Army v. Sandys.

Ayala, Balthazar
 De Jure et Officiis Bellicis et Disciplina Militari Libri III,
 edited by John Westlake. Vol. I, A reproduction of the first
 edition (1582). Vol. II, A translation of the text by John Pawley
 Bate. Baltimore, 1912.

Classical Philology, Vol. 15
 Messer, William Stuart. Mutiny in the Roman Army. The
 Republic, pp. 158-175. Chicago, 1920.

Corpus Inscriptionum Latinarum, Vol. I, pp. 486-545, edited by Theodore
 Mommsen. Berlin, 1863.

Daremberg, Ch. et Saglio, Edm.
 Dictionnaire Des Antiquites Greques et Romaines. Paris,
 1877.

Dodge, Teodore Ayrault
 Caesar. A History of the Art of War among the Romans down
 to the End of the Roman Empire, with a Detailed Account of the
 Campaigns of Caius Julius Caesar. Boston and New York, 1892.

Drumann, William Carl
 Geschichte Roms. Berlin, 1899.

Fortesque, J. W.
 Military History, pp. 176-179. Cambridge and New York,
 1914.

Frölich, Dr. Franz
 Das Kriegwesen Casars, pp. 114-120. Zurich, 1891.

Holmes, Thomas Edward
 Caesar's Conquest of Gaul. London, 1911.

Judson, Harry Pratt
 Caesar's Army, pp. 38-39. Boston, 1888.

Lipsius, Justus
 Justi Lipsi Opera Omnia, Nunc primum copioso rerum indici
 illustrata. Vol. V. Antwerp, 1637.

Mahan, D. H.

Outpost with the Historical Sketch of the Rise and Progress of Tactics, pp. 13-19. New York, 1862.

Marquardt
Romische Staatsverwaltung, Vol. II, pp. 571-593, Das Militarwesen, revised by H. Dessau und A. von Domaszewski. Leipsic, 1887.

McCartney, Eugene S.
Warfare by Land and Sea, Chaps. VIII-IX. Boston, 1923.

Mommsen, Theodore
Historische Schriften. Berlin, 1906.

Pauly
Real-Encyklopädie. Stuttgart, 1864.
Real-Encyklopädie der classischen Altertumswissenschaft herausgegeben von Georg Wissowa. Stuttgart, 1899.

Peter, Carl
Zeittafeln der römischen Geschichte. Halle, 1882.

Rückert, Dr. Fr. W.
Das Römischen Kriegwesen, pp. 40-44. Berlin, 1854.

Sandys, Sir John Edwin
A Companion to Latin Studies, pp. 458-489. Cambridge, 1910.

Schiller, Dr. Herman
Die Kriegsaltertümer (Müllers Handbuch, Vol. IV, pt. 2, pp. 266- 268.) Munich, 1890.

Suidas
Suidae Lexicon ex recognitione Immanuelis Bekkeri. Reimer, 1854.

# Abbreviations Referring to Ancient Authors and Their Works

Ampel.— L. Ampeli Liber Memorialis.

App. — Appians' Roman History, Books I-XII.

     B.C. — Bellum Civile, Books I-IIL

Bell. Afr. — Bellum Africanum (Author uncertain, probably Hirtius).

Bell. Alex. — Bellum Alexandrinum (Author probably Hirtius).

Bell. Hisp. — Bellum Hispaniense (Author uncertain).

Aur. Vic. — Aurelius Victor.

     De Caes. — De Caesaribus.

     Vir. Ill.— De Viris Illustribus.

Caes. — C. Julius Caesar.

     B.C. —Bellum Civile.

     B.G. —Bellum Gallicum.

Cic. — M. Tullius Cicero.

     De Off. —De Offlciis.

     De Fin. — De Finibus.

     Cat. Maj. — De Senectute.

Dig. — Libri Pandectarum Justiniani Digesta.

Dio — Cassius Dio Coccianus' Roman History.

Diod. — Diodorus Siculus' Bibliotheca Historica.

     Fr. — Fragmenta.

Dion. Hal. — Dionysius Halicarnassensis.

     Antiq. Rom. — Antiquitates Romanae.

Eutr. — Flavi Eutropi Breviarum Ab Urbe Condita.

Fest. — Sext. Pompei Festi De Verborum Significatu.

Flor. — L. Annaei Flori Epitomae de T. Livio.

Front. — Julius Frontinus.

     Strat. — Strategematon.

Gell. — Aulus Gellius.

     Noct. Att. — Noctes Atticae.

Justin. — Justini Trogi Pompei Historiarum Philippiacarum Epitoma.

Liv. — T. Livi Ab Urbe Condita Libri.

     Epit. — Epitomae.

Nep. — Cornelius Nepos.

     Hann. — Hannibal.

Oros. — Pauli Orosi Historiae Adversus Paganos.

Obseq. — Julius Obsequens.

     Frag. Ox. — Fragmenta Oxyrhynchi.

Plin. — C. Plini Secundi Historia Naturalis.
Plut. — Plutarch
      Aem. Paul. — Aemilius Paulus.
      Ant. — M. Antonius.
      Apophth. Scip. Min. — Apophthemata Scipionis Minoris.
      Apophth. Reg. et Imp. — Apophthemata Regum et Imperatorum.
      Brut. — Brutus.
      Cam. — Camillus.
      Cato — Cato the Censor.
      Comp. Per. et Fab. — Comparison of Pericles and Fabius.
      Crass. — Crassus.
      Fab. Max. — Fabius Maximus.
      Gracch. — Gracchi.
      Lucull. — Lucullus.
      Mar. — Marius.
      Marcel. — Marcellus.
      Pomp. — Pompeius.
      Pop. — Publicola.
      Pyrrh. — Pyrrhus.
      Ser. — Sertorius.
Polyaen. — Polyaeni Strategematon Libri Octo.
      exc. — excerpta.
Polyb. — Polybius' Histories.
Sall. — C. Sallustius Crispus.
      Jug. — Jugurtha.
Sil. Ital. — C. Sili Italici Punica.
Suet. — C. Suetonius Tranquillus.
      Jul. — Julius.
Tac. — C. Cornelius Tacitus.
      Ann. — Annales.
Val. Max. — Valeri Maximi Factorum et Dictorum Memorabilium Libri.
Varro — M. Terenti Varronis De Lingua Latina.
Veg. —F. Vegetius Renatus.
      Mil. — Epitoma Rei Militaris.
Vell. Pat. — P. Vellei Paterculi Historiae Romanae Libri.
Zon. — Zonaras.

www.ingramcontent.com/pod-product-compliance
Lightning Source LLC
Chambersburg PA
CBHW060814100426
42813CB00004B/1076